Greater is He that is in Me:

You Came, You went, You conquered

Ye are of God, little children, and have overcome them: because greater is he that is in you, than he that is in the world.

1 John 4:4

Be Great!

Tina M Brantley

Tina M Brantley

Table of Contents

Prayer List

Intentionally Left Blank

Acknowledgement

First, I want to thank God for allowing me this opportunity. Without him I am nothing, but with him I am the greatest ME. I thank God for the support of my family, my church, and all of my friends who pushed me on this journey. I truly thank God for my Father and Mother who were my first examples of who Christ is and true representation of God's promised miracles. I especially thank God for those who walked out of my life. One thing I know for sure is that God is a keeper. He is a Keeper of hearts, Keeper of promises and He is a Keeper of truth.

Introduction

God is calling His kingdom to a higher standard. At times, we fail to meet those standards due to difficulties in our daily lives. You may be going through a situation right now, but this is the best time to begin this process. You may be coming out of a situation, and it is still a great time to go through this process. My prior book, *31 Days of Consecration,* is a guide to help you find yourself in the midst of your storm. It guides you to reevaluate decisions, people, and how you see yourself. It separates you from everything that is going on in your life so that you can spend time with and focus on God. The revised and extended version,*You Came, You Went, You Conquered,* will continue help heal, rebuild and enhance your relationship with God through studying and completeing the worksheets. God used the same words (Bible) to save people, no matter how different they are. His word will never change; it is the same today, as it was yesterday and will be forevermore. It is never too late; regardless of how you feel about yourself understand that you are full of greatness.

The Bible says, "You shall consecrate yourselves therefore and be holy, for I am the Lord your God" (Leviticus 20:7). Taking time out to read the devotionals; and answer the questions is a way to bring you closer to God and keep your mind off of your issues. It is a way to serve God and wait upon him. Technically, you are consecrating yourselves because you are created for God's purpose. You are not your own. We were bought with a price--a price so high that no amount of money can settle this bill. This is a continuous process. Philippians 2:13 says "For it is God which worketh in you both to will and to do of *his* good pleasure." This is the time to have a true encounter with God. Stop waiting for God to come rescue you; go to him in your everyday situations.

You must stop waiting for the mantel to come down to you; you have to come up to the mantel. God has higher regards for you and your life. Come up to the mantel that God has for you. Rise higher in your spiritual life so that you can be the person that God needs you to be. Everyone has a spiritual gift from God. God has gifted you and called you, so allow God to direct you to the right path that will lead you to your gift.

Change is a process that requires a great deal of patience. God will reveal what He wants you to know about the people in your life and yourself. When God begins to reveal who you really are, do not be surprised if it is not a pretty revelation. Some of the ugliest parts of our lives are the pieces of the person that you see in the mirror every day. To build a healthy relationship, one has to get

Who is around you? There are people who will help you row the boat. There are people who will rock the boat. There are people who will cheer you on. There are people who will motivate you to get out the boat. There are some that will discourage you from getting out the boat. Who are you attached to? Who are you connected to? Know who is around you.

rid of all of the mess. There is a purpose behind your pain, your problems, and your sickness. Understand that God uses your problems to help shield you from greater harm.

There were several examples of consecration in the Bible. For example, in Joshua 3:5, after the people of Israel wandered through the wilderness for 40 years; they were commanded to consecrate themselves before they were able to enter the Promised Land. God needs you to be emptied, cleansed, and purified before he is able to fill you up and fulfill his promise within you. You cannot pour new wine into old wineskin; because both will be ruined.

Luke 9:23 states, "If any man will come after Me, let him deny himself, and take up his cross DAILY, and follow Me." Give God your all; set aside alone time for you and Him in order to build a relationship. Allow God to refine your heart and improve your life within Him. You are great, and you can only know how great you are when you have a personal relationship with God. Prepare to be used by God. Your time is now.

How to get started:

You have to set aside time to focus on what God needs you to do. Change does not come easy, but it will help develop you into the greatest person you can be; nevertheless, you have to do it with God. Get into the presence of God by following these four steps: praise and worship, prayer, study and meditation, and journaling. Set aside time each day, preferably at least 60 minutes or until God releases you, engaging in the four steps. You will need your music, Bible, journal, and a designated place for your private time with God. This should be a place where you will not be distracted. During your set aside time, you will also fast-- only consume water. Make sure you journal your experiences. Journal each day following your designated time to ensure that your mind is still fresh. Make sure you are comfortable and stay focused so that you may hear from God and communicate with God. Before starting your consecration consider these preliminary steps:

1. Repent of your sins.
    a. Confess those things to God. You want to start with a clean slate.
2. Leave all your burdens with God.
    a. There is no sense in carrying those burdens into the process of change. It will only hinder you from pressing forward.
3. Ask God to purify your heart.

a. You must be honest with God in what you want. You must first desire for God to purify your heart to ensure you never go back to who you were. Ask him to change the way you think and how your heart feels. You can only do this with the help of God.

4. Ask God to help you stay committed
   a. Once you have laid down your burdens and asked God to purify your heart, ask him to help you stay committed to the process of change. This part will take a great deal of work on your end. God can only do what you allow him to do, so stay committed.

5. Ask God to help you draw closer to him
   a. This is the purpose of your change, to draw closer to God. The closer you are to him the easier it can be to stay focused. Like the old folks used to say, "Jesus keep me near the cross." Everything that you need will be at the cross, at the feet of Jesus.

Praise and Worship: This is a way to usher in the presence of the Lord. When you begin your consecration, each day you will want to clear your mind of all issues and daily activity. Play your favorite songs, or if you prefer to sing, sing them.

Prayer: Before you open the word of God or begin to read your daily motivation, pray. Ask God to reveal things that are not of Him so that they will be removed. Understand that more than half of your consecration will be praying. Pray your prayer to God.

Study and Meditation: Begin to study and meditate on the word of the day.

Journal and workbook: It is best to write in your journal immediately after the experience is over for that day. This will ensure that you capture the information while it is still fresh in your mind. Meditate on the questions and answer them truthfully. This is all about making yourselve greater with God.

Opening Prayer

God, I come into agreement that there will be an encounter with you during this journey of getting closer to you. I pray that this will be a life changing experience where issues will be demolished. Hearts will be mended, problems will be solved, addictions will cease and sins will be cleared. I pray that the focus will be on You. God, begin to transform the life of the person reading this and give them the hope to continue this journey. I declare and decree that his or her life will never be the same. After this encounter, he or she will see you much clearer dear God. Fill this individual with your glory; fill him or her with your power so he or she can pour into others. Bring about an overflow of knowledge and understanding God. God, we have come to you just as we are. We have gone forth with your word and we will conquer in your name. So, Father we humbly surrender all that we are to You and only you in Jesus' name. Amen.

Message from the Author- I stand in agreement with you

I declare and decree that amazing things are going to happen after your encounter with God. I guarantee you will be a greater person. You will no longer be the same. Each person's experience will be different, but please make sure you have an intimate experience with God. This process can get very intense; make sure you devote yourself to meeting with God daily. This is just a guide to give you motivation, encouragement, and help you study. You know your issues and the things you need to correct, so stay focused. Go beyond the scriptures that are given. I celebrate you in advance for taking this step to enhance your life. Remember that YOU ARE GREAT so begin to live and act like it. You came, you went, and you conquered.

My Story

I was at the lowest point in my life. I had just gotten out of a long-term relationship, my only relationship, and this was all I knew at the age of 31. I had to break the cycle in my life to keep me from running back to a situation that was not good for my soul. I was in a new city with no family and no friends so the only person I had to trust and call on was God. One day while in church, I heard the pastor talking about consecration. Growing up, I'd never heard of consecration, so I didn't understand what it meant. Based on some research that I conducted, I decided to give it a try. I not only wanted to consecrate myself to have a closer relationship with God, but I also wanted to get rid of some of my strongholds and soul ties. The consecration came at the worst time in my life, so I was desperate for change.

The consecration was very intense for me because I decided to fast from the things I wanted to separate myself from. Those things consisted of my ex (who was my biggest issue), unworthy friends, my mouth (ex. cursing, gossiping, and being rude), and low self-esteem. During this time, I learned that some people would not understand why I embarked on this journey or why I "traveled" alone, but I had to do what was going to make me great in God. You may ask, "How did you fast from low self-esteem and your mouth. Only emotional and mental issues contributed to my low self-esteem, not physical issues, so I learned to trust and love myself. I spoke good things about myself whenever I looked in the mirror. I fasted from my mouth by not habitually speaking negative things into my life; I spoke only positively even if I didn't feel like it. Yes, the negative speech was my "normal" at that time. I was determined to become a better me.

There were times I wasn't in the mood and did not want to go through the process, or I wanted to give up, but I had to fight my way through the process. The process of healing is not easy. If you want relief, you have to release the pain in order to revive your heart. It is never good to carry old hurt and emotion into a new situation. The waiting process for change was long, but the healing and the peace were worth the wait.

When I felt like giving up, God revealed himself to me.

During this process, God revealed several things and people to me. The most important revelation I received was when God revealed myself to me. It was not a pretty sight. I remember being mad at God, but I still consecrated at my set aside time for three days. I didn't speak, pray or read my Bible because I was angry, but I did sit and mediate on what God showed me. I could not handle the ugly parts of me.

Before we can truly change who we are, we must first be confronted with and understand who we truly are. God is the best examiner I know.

When I finally accepted my ugly truth, I looked it right in the face. I told myself, "I refuse to be you any longer. I will no longer be a carbon copy of sin. I am going to be who God made me."

Example of journal entry

Day 2   God Revealed Me   07/25/2012
Judges: 15-17

Going into day 2 I was almost tempted not to do it, but I got excited the closer it got to 7 pm. I started with worship, prayer, and meditation. God lead me to read Judges 15. This revealed more about me. It was talking about Samson and how Delilah deceived him. At that moment, he could not see through her lies due to being blinded by lust. I know God is preparing me for something because of the things I have been through. In my life application study bible, it asked a question, "How can you keep your desire for love and sexual pleasure from deceiving you?"

1. You have to decide what type of person you will love before the passion takes over. Then, you have to determine if the person's character and faith in God are as pleasing as their physical appearance.

2. Most of the time you spend with your spouse will not include sex.

3. Be patient. Time and observation often reveal what is beneath the pleasant appearance and attentive touch.

Samson allowed himself to become weak to Delilah's nagging and he gave in to her request. I have to remember to never allow anyone to tempt me regardless of how attractive, persuasive, or persistent he or she is. These scriptures helped to reveal how vulnerable I was to love. I am learning to be patient. I need to avoid falling prey to deceit by asking God to help me distinguish between deception and truth. This is something I asked God about months ago and He has allowed people to drop out of my life. Now it's about releasing the people that I want in my life that are not supposed to be here. I have chosen to start over and get closer to God rather than go my own way. It's not worth the consequences.

Samson became spiritually blind and without strength. THIS WAS ME. I was bound to a relationship for over 14 years and I didn't have the strength to leave; I felt like a slave. I know God can still work in my situation, because He worked in Samson's. He answered Samson's prayer even after he sinned. I can be saved if I am willing to repent and come back to God. This revelation was not pretty.

Later that night after meditation I wrote:

I ended this consecration night around 9:45 pm because it was all I could handle. I was angry at myself and I just broke down because I never saw myself in that aspect. I felt as if I was weak and gullible. I know God is revealing me to myself in order to make me better. I had to consult my spiritual leader because I was a mess, and I was so angry at God. I thought I had it all together, but He showed me the true me and I couldn't handle it. I am worried about what He will reveal next, but I have to continue. I know the reward will be great.

End of journal

When we see ourselves as perfect and everyone else as imperfect, God has a way of showing us that we are no different. That is what was displayed about Tina. I was so angry at God that it took me 3 days to get over this revelation. Wow! Although I still did my consecration, it was merely quiet time in the presence of the Lord. I would just lie on my bed and just think of him. God did not reveal these things to hurt me but to make me better. That is what consecration is about. I wasn't prepared for the outcome. I also realized during this process that when God is great in me, I am displaying a greater me.

1 John 4:4 "Ye are of God, little children, and have overcome them: because greater is he that is in you, than he that is in the world."

Your Journey Begins…

1

Building a Closer Relationship

◈ · ◈

Psalm 139:7-14

"For You formed my inward parts; you covered me in my mother's womb. I will praise you, for I am fearfully and wonderfully made; marvelous are your works, and that my soul knows very well."

Jeremiah 29:11

"For I know the plans I have for you," declares the LORD, "plans to prosper you and not to harm you, plans to give you hope and a future."

Relationships are extremely important when it comes to building connections or simply getting to know someone. To build a relationship, there must be communication, especially when it comes to our faith. The only way you can truly know God is by having a personal relationship with him. This means you should set apart an appointed time to have direct communication with God. You have an open line with God to communicate anything you want to communicate -- the windows of heaven are open. He speaks to you through the word and the Holy Spirit. When building a relationship with God, understand that He knew you before you were created. What better person to have a relationship with than that one who has fearfully and wonderfully created you? God is concerned about those things that concern you. Get to know him so you can follow his plan for your life. The first record of a relationship goes back to Genesis, which is the relationship between God and man. Get to know who you are in God so that you can be the greatest you.

Prayer

God, I ask you to guide me and draw me closer to you. For you know the plans of my life, and I want to get to know you.

Do you understand the relationship between God and Man? Explain.

_____

_____

_____

_____

_____

Evaluate your relationship with God. Date_____

_____

_____

_____

_____

_____

_____

_____

In 30 days re-evaluate your relationship. How has it changed? How do you feel? Has it affected the decisions you make?

_____

_____

_____

_____

_____

_____

_____

2

Repent

Acts 3:19

"Repent, therefore, and turn back, that your sins may be blotted out."

Acts 11:19

"When they heard this, they had no further objections and praised God, saying, So then, even to Gentiles God has granted repentance that leads to life."

God has given us all of the tools to do what it takes in our life. The first item is the ability to repent. In order, to be saved one must repent and confess their sins. Scripture states, "To have your sins removed, you have to turn back to God." You have to humble yourselves unto God, and once you are convicted for the sins you have committed, you must change your behavior. God is ordering us to turn from sin today. On this journey make sure the principle of repentance becomes embedded in your head. Understand that when you repent, there is an action that has to follow; there must be a change in behavior.

On this day be sure to focus on anything that you need to repent for. We want to start with a clean slate.

Prayer

God, I am asking You to forgive me for all of my sins. Forgive me for all the sins that I am both aware and unaware of so that I can begin this journey to greatness. I am turning back to You, and I will conform to Your will.

Find biblical stories that include someone repenting of his or her sin(s). What was the outcome?

_____
_____
_____
_____
_____
_____
_____

Read the story of Adam and Eve. What may have happened if Adam would have repented?

_____
_____
_____
_____
_____
_____
_____

Reflect over the last three months: Have you repented for all the sins you may have committed known and unknown?

Yes   No

☐   ☐

_____
_____
_____
_____
_____
_____
_____

3

The Answer is Yes

2 Corinthians 1:20-22

"For no matter how many promises God has made, they are "Yes" in Christ. And so through him the "Amen" is spoken by us to the glory of God. [21] Now it is God who makes both us and you stand firm in Christ. He anointed us, [22] set his seal of ownership on us, and put his Spirit in our hearts as a deposit, guaranteeing what is to come."

The answer is simply "yes," a "yes" to His will and a "yes" to His way. There are times we may not say "yes" to God or we may say "yes" with our mouths, but our actions display something different. We have to give God a solid "yes" followed by behavioral changes and action.

Have you ever had one of those moments where you were rebellious? You know that God is telling you to do something, but you constantly tell him "NO." Then you begin to notice that the situation gets a little harder or worse. When you finally decide to tell Him "yes" it feels like a huge weight has lifted and things start to get better.

As a member of the Kingdom of God, He will not tell you to do something that will harm you. We have to watch what we say "no" to because it can put us so deep into a bad situation that we can possibly separate ourselves from God. Just because you may not like what God is telling you to do, it doesn't mean God is going to pull back. That mission is for you and your purpose. Make sure that your answers are "yes."

Reflection: What if Jesus said "no?"

What are some things that you are saying "yes" to?

_____

_____

_____

_____

_____

_____

Name some things you can do to keep your promise to God.

_____

_____

_____

_____

_____

We know that God's "yes" is sufficient, but is your "yes" circumstantial?

_____

_____

_____

_____

_____

_____

_____

4

Dependent Prayer

Matthew 6:9-13

"After this manner therefore pray ye: 'Our Father which art in heaven, Hallowed be thy name. Thy kingdom come, Thy will be done in earth, as it is in heaven. Give us this day our daily bread. And forgive us our debts, as we forgive our debtors. And lead us not into temptation, but deliver us from evil: For thine is the kingdom, and the power, and the glory, forever. Amen.' "

Praying is one of the keys to building a relationship with God. Learn to pray without ceasing. Don't be so easy to give up if you don't feel God's presence immediately. God has already made clear that our prayers are important to Him. He says, "Then you will call upon me and come and pray to me, and I will listen to you. You will seek me and find me when you search for me with all your heart" (Jeremiah 29:13).

When you are in prayer about a particular issue always find a scripture, and stand on it. Stand on the word of God for that vision, dream, healing or whatever you are praying about. It says in Matthew, "Whatever you ask in prayer believe and you shall receive it."

Often we think that we are too dirty to pray or too dirty to seek him, because we are ashamed of our sins. This is when God wants you the most. There are times people will intercede for others, but not themselves. It is time out for the shame; you cannot become God's greatest masterpiece until you begin to work on you. Cover yourselves so that you can intercede for others. Prayer is essential to your relationship with God. You have to be like Nehemiah and develop a relationship with God that is dependent upon Him. I heard a speaker say, "Prayer is warfare to the last breath." It is a part of your deliverance. The prayers of the righteous availeth much.

Exercise: Spend a tenth of each hour of your day to pray (these are the hours you are awake). It doesn't matter where you are or what you are doing. If you are in the grocery store, say a prayer. It can be as little as *"thank you, God,"* but get into the habit of talking to him on a regular basis.

Read **Ephesians 3:14-21**. What are the four points of Paul's prayer? Explain

_____
_____
_____
_____
_____
_____
_____
_____
_____
_____

Create your own four points of prayer

1._____
_____

2._____
_____

3._____
_____

4._____
_____

5

Understanding Your Purpose

Exodus 9:16

"But I have raised you up for this very purpose, that I might show you my power and that my name might be proclaimed in all the earth."

Proverbs 19:20

"Many are the plans in a person's heart, but it is the Lord's purpose that prevails."

Proverb 20:5

"The purposes of a person's heart are deep waters, but one who has insight draws them out."

Job 42:2

"I know that I can do all things; no purpose of yours can be thwarted."

Every so often, after we have our first encounter with God or we have been with God for some time we tend to ask, "What is my purpose?" God has a plan for everyone's life. Do not compromise God's purpose for you by assuming and doing just anything. Ask God what your purpose is. In order to know the purpose God has for you, you must develop a relationship with Him and be obedient. So many people walk around and feel as if they have no purpose in the kingdom, but that is far from the truth. God's purpose for you is so much greater than any dream or wish.

When God has a purpose for you, He will lead you to the right people. Those right people can help push you towards your destiny and to your purpose. The right connections will allow you to stand in front of millions. There are going to be people who say you are not good enough, but God says you are better than enough. We have to understand that it's not about who you know on earth, it's about the God you know. Moses wasn't a good speaker, but yet God had a purpose for him and that was to free the people in Egypt.

When you are living in your God-given purpose you will experience different types of feelings. The devil will try to destroy your family and your friends. People will turn their backs on you and speak negative things about you. There will be several things that will try to come against you, but if you are living your   God-given purpose, He will see you through it. No man or devil can tear it apart.

While you are living your purpose, there are going to be people around you who are specifically designed to help you fulfill your purpose. They will lead the right people. God sometimes, however, allows us to operate in our own purpose. For instance, if you want to be a writer you can, but it may not be God's purpose for your life. Although something may be your heart's desire, do not allow it to get in the way of God's purpose for your life.

Do you know your purpose? Explain.

_____
_____
_____
_____
_____
_____
_____

Does your purpose align with God's purpose for your life?

_____
_____
_____
_____
_____
_____
_____

"But I have raised you up for this very purpose, that I might show you my power and that my name might be proclaimed in all the earth" **Exodus 9:16**

What does **Exodus 9:16** mean to you?

_____
_____
_____
_____
_____
_____

How can your purpose elevate your life?

_____
_____
_____
_____
_____

6

Stay Hungry & Thirsty for God

◈ · ◈

Matthew 5:6

"Blessed are they which do hunger and thirst after righteousness: for they shall be filled."

John 7:37

"On the last and greatest day of the festival, Jesus stood and said in a loud voice, 'Let anyone who is thirsty come to me and drink.' "

Once you have been a believer for some time and have experienced ups and down, you will begin to feel parched. There are going to be times when you don't feel God, and you may have even stopped chasing Him or thirsting after Him. You must stay thirsty for God. Continue to chase Him and continue to want more of Him. If you are empty, seek God to fill you up with more of Him. If you do not stay hungry or thirsty for God you can fall back into your old lifestyle. If you continue to seek Him, study and pray, then He will ensure you are fed with the right resources. God wants greater for you; therefore, you must press your way through the war to keep the fire for God burning.

When you thirst after God, make sure you drink from the right well, which is God's well. Every well isn't good for you. You have to use discernment on what well you get your information from. God will lead you to the living water, but He will not force you to drink it. If you want to be filled with the Lord, you must drink from Him. Life will sometimes drain or dehydrate you, and oftentimes it will never satisfy your needs. This is why you need to thirst after God's well and only then will it fill you up until you are overflowing.

Thirst more, chase more and stay focused. Get rid of any substitutes because you will not have an appetite for Him if you are being satisfied by something else. Stop snacking on fleshly and worldly things so that you can receive the banquet that God has laid before you.

Continue to long for His presence like a thirsty person in a desert longing for water.

Reflect: Do not allow your physical thirst to get in the way of your spiritual thirst. Physical thirst can bring different types of changes, even death. However, spiritual thirst can save your life. Think of anything that you physically thirst over and ask God to help you dehydrate those thirsts and enhance your spiritual thirst.

List any of your thirsts that are not of God. Then list different ways to dehydrate that thirst.

Thirst	**Dehydration**
_____	_____
_____	_____
_____	_____
_____	_____
_____	_____
_____	_____
_____	_____
_____	_____
_____	_____
_____	_____
_____	_____
_____	_____
_____	_____
_____	_____
_____	_____
_____	_____
_____	_____

7

Fight, Press on, and Do not be Defeated

◈ . . . . ◈

Ephesians 6:10-20

"[10] Finally, be strong in the Lord and in his mighty power. [11] Put on the full armor of God, so that you can take your stand against the devil's schemes. [12] For our struggle is not against flesh and blood, but against the rulers, against the authorities, against the powers of this dark world and against the spiritual forces of evil in the heavenly realms. [13] Therefore put on the full armor of God, so that when the day of evil comes, you may be able to stand your ground, and after you have done everything, to stand. [14] Stand firm then, with the belt of truth buckled around your waist, with the breastplate of righteousness in place, [15] and with your feet fitted with the readiness that comes from the gospel of peace. [16] In addition to all this, take up the shield of faith, with which you can extinguish all the flaming arrows of the evil one. [17] Take the helmet of salvation and the sword of the Spirit, which is the word of God.

[18] And pray in the Spirit on all occasions with all kinds of prayers and requests. With this in mind, be alert and always keep on praying for all the Lord's people. [19] Pray also for me, that whenever I speak, words may be given me so that I will fearlessly make known the mystery of the gospel, [20] for which I am an ambassador in chains. Pray that I may declare it fearlessly, as I should."

During the desperate fight for your life, you will go through the wilderness just as others may go through floodwaters. Is there a murky and contaminated situation going on in your life? Are you wondering who will rescue you? Are you waving your white flag? Are you ready to give up on this battle? You may be ready to throw in the towel because your back is against the wall, but God says I have equipped you for what I called you to do. You have to press on; do not be defeated. I have given you the full armor to protect you in these tough situations." In Luke 1:37, it says, "for with God nothing shall be impossible."

The fight will not be easy. It will take your full faith and your full ability to stand and rest in the storm. Yes, RESTING in the storm is still a way to fight and not be defeated. As the storm came and Jesus was in the boat asleep, the disciples were worried and wondering how He could sleep during a storm that was so vicious? Do not allow the storm to rough you up, or worry you; you will not be defeated. As long as you keep Jesus with you, there is nothing to worry about.

God has anointed you to fight and conquer. Always remember 2 Corinthians 12:10, "That is why, for Christ's sake, I delight in weaknesses, in insults, in hardships, in persecutions, and in difficulties. For when I am weak, then I am strong. When we are weak within ourselves, then we are strong in the grace of the Lord. In our weakness, God's strength is made perfect. God is glorified in our trials. Don't allow the enemy to be magnified or glorified by allowing him to win. We allow him to win when we don't call on the name of Jesus in our trials. Put your trust in the most high God.

Jesus was speaking to Peter when he said, "Satan has a desire to sift you as weak, but I am praying that your faith will fail you not." Your faith will not fail you even in your trying times your tribulations. You will not grow weary in your well-doing. You will reap your harvest in due season if you do not faint. Just know it is in the pressing.

How strong is your endurance?

_____
_____
_____
_____
_____
_____
_____

How did you fight your last fight? Was it fought
spiritually or physically?

_____
_____
_____
_____
_____
_____
_____

How did you feel after the fight?

_____
_____
_____
_____
_____
_____
_____

Was your relationship with God stronger?

_____
_____
_____
_____
_____
_____
_____

8

In & Out of Season/ Seen and Unseen

2 Timothy 4:2

"Preach the word; be ready in season and out of season; reprove, rebuke, and exhort, with complete patience and teaching."

Continuing the work of the kingdom can definitely be a challenge considering the day-to-day obstacles. Press your way through adversity even if you don't feel like it. God simply asks you to preach His word in season and out of season--when you are feeling good and when you are feeling bad. Your purpose is to glorify God through it all. We all hit some rough patches, but God sees your work and you will be rewarded for pressing on. There are so many people who will only work to be seen, but God is calling forth true children of God who are able to continue to do the work when no one sees them. Is your faith the same when no one sees you doing the good work or preaching the word of God? God is looking for faithful servants who do not need a title or a platform to worship His name.

Whether we feel like it or not we should always be ready to do what God has called us to do. We cannot allow ourselves to be unemployable in the spiritual realm, so from this day forward do not have any limited seasons. What if God limited your blessings? Or what if God only blessed you based on the work you do? What would your blessings look like? Do not be unbalanced, be ready. If you are a soldier in the army, you have to always be alert and ready for battle, even in the middle of the night when you are supposed to be asleep. God's work never stops. If you are not prepared, the devil can ambush you at any time.

The best way to stay ready is through prayer, studying, and spending personal time with God. Do not only fight the convenient and easy fights, but fight all fights in season and out of season, seen and unseen. Victory is never obtained easily.

Think: If someone approached you today and asked you why should they give their life to Christ would you be ready to answer? And would you answer according to God's word? Remember good deeds are to be performed, not preached.

Has there ever been a time when you felt overwhelmed and God presented someone for you to minister to, but you didn't feel like ministering?

_____

_____

_____

_____

_____

_____

Have you ever missed a chance to minister God's word to a person?

_____

_____

_____

_____

_____

_____

How did your decisions affect you?

_____

_____

_____

_____

_____

_____

How do you stay ready to do the work of God?

_____

_____

_____

_____

_____

_____

9

Understand you are Safe in His Arms

◈ · · · · · · · · · · · · · · · · · · ◈

Joshua 23:8

"But you are to hold fast to the LORD your God, as you have until now."

2 Timothy 4:17-18

"[17] But the Lord stood at my side and gave me strength, so that through me the message might be fully proclaimed and all the Gentiles might hear it. And I was delivered from the lion's mouth. [18] The Lord will rescue me from every evil attack and will bring me safely to his heavenly kingdom. To him be glory for ever and ever. Amen. "

Have you ever depended on a person or a family member that you trusted? Was this individual the type of person who would allow you to cry on his or her shoulder and always ensured that you were safe? Did you believe that everything you told him or her was safe, but later issues developed and you discovered that your friend or your family member was not the safe haven you thought they would be in your time of need? The devil will try to destroy you when you feel unsafe. The strategy of the devil is to confuse you and put fear in your heart. The devil wants you to think that you have no one to turn to. He will drag you into a dark place where you feel alone.

Understand that in every situation God has you wrapped in his arms. Problems may be overwhelming, but you have to cling to God. Joshua told the people of Israel to cling to the Lord your God. Don't cling to man or material things, only God. God knows how to keep you because you are not fit to keep yourself. God is calling you to shift your dependency on Him. It is okay to rest in Jesus. Stop worrying because you are safe. Hardships will come, but you have Him to rest on. When you find yourself in a storm, always remember who is in the boat with you. When you are in the midst of your storm, turn to God. Safe means "to protect, not expose to danger, or risk to be harmed or injured."

God will not leave you or forsake you. The words He speaks over your life will not come back null or void. Rest easy in God.

Exercise: On this day lay all of your burdens down. This includes your children, your job, your bills, your church, yourself, etc. This should be a worry free evening and all I want you to do is rest. Rest in his presence and meditate on the goodness of the Lord.

What did you experience when you finally laid all of your burdens down?

_____

_____

_____

_____

_____

_____

_____

_____

_____

_____

_____

_____

_____

_____

_____

_____

_____

_____

_____

_____

_____

_____

10

Faith and Trust

2 Corinthians 5:7

"For we walk by faith, not by sight"

Proverbs 3:5

"Trust in the LORD with all thine heart, and lean not unto thine own understanding."

Visual Interaction

Close your eyes and imagine you are standing on a cliff. God has already told you, "Never go back and never look back. What is behind you will not and cannot hinder you as long as you have faith and keep your eyes on me." As you are standing on the cliff there is nothing ahead of you, but you know you have to keep going, you have to press, and you have to push. Stop…because you are too busy trying to figure out how to get to the other side, or you are trying to understand why you must get to the other side, this way.

Now envision God telling you, "You don't always have to know how or understand why, just have the faith of a mustard seed and know that I will carry you to the other side."

With your eyes still closed, begin to build your faith, and step off of the cliff. Continue to focus on God just like Peter did when he walked on the water. Don't look up, don't look down, don't look to the side, and don't look back. Stay focused on what is ahead. As long as you keep your focus on Him, every step that you take will be on solid ground, even if you can't see or feel it.

There are going to be times in your life when you lose faith, fall in midair (in the middle of your issue), and find yourself in the valley. Understand that God is in the valley with you. You just need to pick yourself up, rebuild your faith, and continue to walk until you get back to where you belong. Once you are able to get back up, continue to walk forward. God has ordered your steps according to His will. As long as you follow Him you will make it to the other side.

Along this journey, you will run into some hurdles (test and trials), but you must activate your faith and continue to walk. God never said it was going to be easy. You may have to go to war and come out with some scars, cuts, and bruises, but continue to walk because God has secured the battle. You may run into some naysayers, backbiters, gossipers, dream killers, but stay focused and keep walking. Storms may come and the water may be troubled, but keep walking. The devil may be trying to take you out, but keep walking, rebuke him and seal the rebuke with the blood of the lamb in the name of Jesus Christ.

Your family may turn their backs on you, your church members may hurt you, or try to discredit your character, but you must stay focused on God and KEEP walking. Sickness may show up, but you know that God is a healer--keep walking; you may be financially unstable, but know that God is a provider--keep walking. You may be homeless, but you know that God will provide shelter--keep walking. Your house or your marriage may be in shambles, but you know that God is a mender and He can put anything back together again, so keep walking. You may begin to lose confidence, have doubts, and see yourself as a failure, but God says, "You are a winner, you are the head and not the tail, you are a conqueror." Stay focused and keep walking.

No matter the issue, no matter the situation or trial, stay focused on God and keep walking.

Once you get close to the other side, you will begin to feel a breakthrough. Know that your blessing is on the way due to the hardships you endured. Because of your faith and trust in God, you will finally make it to your breakthrough. This is the real meaning of "walk by faith and not by sight." If you keep your physical eyes open along the journey, you will be distracted, but if you use your spiritual eyes (faith), you will trust God, stay focused, make it to your breakthrough, and reach to your destiny on the other side of the cliff.

11

Release to have Relief in Order to be Revived

Psalm 51:10

"Create in me a clean heart, O God; and renew a right spirit within me."

2 Corinthians 5:17

"Therefore if any man be in Christ, he is a new creature: old things are passed away; behold, all things are become new."

Romans 8:28

"And we know that all things work together for good to them that love God, to them who are the called according to his purpose."

Let go and let God. God cannot produce a better you if you keep holding on to old things. Let go of the people who hurt you. There are some people who still carry hurt that happened to them as a child or as a young adult. These people are stuck and cannot receive the full benefits of the life that God wants them to have. It is time to RELEASE: release pain, release anger, release abuse, release the abuser, release drugs, release your father, release your mother, release any family member who has hurt you in any way--Release. God cannot heal what YOU WON'T release. Give God all your hurt and unforgiveness so that you can receive relief.

Once you have released your problems, God will give you relief so He can begin the revitalization process which will lead to the greatest you. God will remove the blocks in your life, but you still have to do your part. There will be a new release of God's anointing in your life. For instance, after the citizens of Rome turned on Paul and Silas, the Roman officials beat and imprisoned them. Instead of being angry, blaming others or holding grudges, Paul and Silas decided to give the issue to God. While in prison they prayed and sang hymns to God and God delivered them that same night. God may not deliver you from your issue as fast as He delivered Paul and Silas, but remain focused on releasing the issue to Him in order for you to be relieved and REVIVED.

1. God will not heal what you won't release.

    a. Don't expect God to move if you will not move. For example, how can God bring you the mate He has made in his image if you have not stopped fornicating or released yourself from the issues of your past relationships?

2. Pour yourself out unto God.

   a. Once you have released yourself, pour yourself out unto God. Give Him all of you. He will then begin the cleansing process. This will be the toughest part of the process because you have to face your issues and circumstances. There will be a great deal of pressure and pushing but it's all for your relief.

3. Release will bring relief so you can be revived.

   a. When you fully release your burdens to God, you will experience a feeling of relief, which feels similar to weight being physically lifted from your body. At that point, you will finally be revived, able to move past the situation that had you bound for so long.

Are there things that you are holding on to that you need to release?

_____
_____
_____
_____
_____
_____
_____
_____

Do you believe that if you release the things that you've been holding on to, God will revive things in your life?

_____
_____
_____
_____
_____
_____
_____
_____

What does RELEASE mean to you?

R_____

E_____

L_____

E_____

A_____

S_____

E_____

12

Study to Show Yourself Approved: Conditioning

2 Timothy 2:15

"Study to show thyself approved unto God, a workman that needeth not to be ashamed, rightly dividing the word of truth."

2 Timothy 3:15-17

[15] "and how from infancy you have known the Holy Scriptures, which are able to make you wise for salvation through faith in Christ Jesus. [16] All Scripture is God-breathed and is useful for teaching, rebuking, correcting and training in righteousness, [17] so that the servant of God may be thoroughly equipped for every good work."

To run a race, you have to condition yourself. A runner will go through a series of workouts and practice runs prior to a race. They will also wear the proper clothing to assure that they can move swiftly. Why do we think working for God is any different? You must be conditioned to win souls. You must study so that you can prove to God you are ready to approach His people or that you are ready to be elevated in the kingdom and in your personal life. You must study to ensure you are prepared to handle anything that the enemy throws at you. you must be ready for anything.

To receive your degree from a college, you must study to pass the test. You must also study to pass God's test and to gain spiritual growth. You will receive understanding and knowledge, but you cannot just pick up the Bible and read the passages. You must examine the Word and apply it to your life. Understand that the race is not given to the swift, nor to the strong, but to the one who endureth. The only way you can endure the race is to study God's Word.

How would you rate your studying?

1	2	3	4	5
O	O	O	O	O
Weak				Strong

If you are not where you want to be with your studying, use the chart below and rate where you would rather be.

1	2	3	4	5
O	O	O	O	O
Weak				Strong

Based on your current rating, could you stand in the midst of a storm? Based on your current rating, could you standup to the devil?

_____

_____

_____

_____

_____

_____

Based on your current rating, could you stand up to the enemy that is spreading lies about your character?

_____

_____

_____

13

Worship, Worship, Worship

◆ · ◆

John 4:20-24

[20] "Our fathers worshipped in this mountain; and ye say, that in Jerusalem is the place where men ought to worship. [21] Jesus saith unto her, Woman, believe me, the hour cometh, when ye shall neither in this mountain, nor yet at Jerusalem, worship the Father. [22] Ye worship ye know not what: we know what we worship: for salvation is of the Jews. [23] But the hour cometh, and now is, when the true worshippers shall worship the Father in spirit and in truth: for the Father seeketh such to worship him. [24] God is a Spirit: and they that worship him must worship him in spirit and in truth."

As a child of God, you were created to worship Him. There are times when you will just have to bow down at the throne of the Lord and worship. The scriptures prove that it doesn't matter where you are, you can worship God in spirit, in truth and in any position. The Bible talks about several ways to worship God:

Standing (1 Kings 8:22), bowing (2 chronicles 20:18), kneeling (Psalms 95:6), shouting (Ps 32:11), dancing (1 Chronicles 15:29), laughing (Ps 126:2), with a loud voice (Lk 17:15-16), with hands held high (Ps 63:4), with a song of praise (40:3), with instruments (Ps 150:3-5), clapping your hands (Ps 47:1), with reverence (Ps 2:11), and prostrating yourself (1 Corinthians 14:24-25).

With all the different ways to worship God, you should never have an excuse not to worship. Your worship will bring about deliverance when you enter the spirit realm God will set you free. Worship God when you are on the mountain top and when you are in the valley. When I was young, I was always told, "It's hard to stumble when you are down on your knees." So, worship God through it all, even when you don't feel Him or even if you don't feel like worshipping Him.

Exercise: This evening focus on giving God your purest worship.

Read **Hebrews 13:15**. What is it saying?

_____

_____

_____

_____

_____

_____

_____

Read **Psalm 47**. What does it mean to you?

_____

_____

_____

_____

_____

_____

_____

_____

Read **Psalm 96**. Explain the different ways to worship.

_____

_____

_____

_____

_____

_____

_____

_____

Begin to walk in your worship each day

PRAISE YOUR WAY THROUGH THE GATES AND
WORSHIP YOUR WAY TO HIS FEET

T.M. BRANTLEY

14

Get Rid of the Old: Make Room for your Blessing

2 Kings 4:8-17

8 "One day Elisha went to Shunem. And a well-to-do woman was there, who urged him to stay for a meal. So whenever he came by, he stopped there to eat. 9 She said to her husband, "I know that this man who often comes our way is a holy man of God. 10 Let's make a small room on the roof and put in it a bed and a table, a chair and a lamp for him. Then he can stay there whenever he comes to us."

11 "One day when Elisha came, he went up to his room and lay down there. 12 He said to his servant Gehazi, "Call the Shunammite." So he called her, and she stood before him. 13 Elisha said to him, "Tell her, 'You have gone to all this trouble for us. Now what can be done for you? Can we speak on your behalf to the king or the commander of the army? She replied, "I have a home among my own people."14 "What can be done for her?" Elisha asked. Gehazi said, "She has no son, and her husband is old." 15 Then Elisha said, "Call her." So he called her, and she stood in the doorway. 16 "About this time next year," Elisha said, "you will hold a son in your arms." "No, my lord!" she objected. "Please, man of God, don't mislead your servant!" 17 But the woman became pregnant, and the next year about that same time she gave birth to a son, just as Elisha had told her."

Today is the day that you must clean out your closet. Clean your closet to make room for all of the things that God wants to present you with. I'm sure there are people like me that have a closet full of old clothes and shoes that are too small. We are hoping and wishing one day that we will get back into those clothes.

We must face our truth that we may not get back into those clothes. This is the same thing we do with people, old dreams, and things that will hold us back. God wants to bless you tremendously, but you must first make room for your blessing. The blessings will not all be monetary or materialistic, but they may be knowledge, wisdom, or new opportunities. You must remove the things that are taking up space. Get rid of the old, dead, and tired things so that God can bring new life.

When I think of making room, I think of the Shunammite woman. Elisha passed by her house often and would occasionally stop by for a meal. One day, the woman asked her husband to build a room for the man of God, so he could stay overnight and rest while he was on his journey. Her generosity touched Elisha, and he asked her, "What can I do for you? You've gone to all this trouble for me, now what can I do for you?" Although she stated there was nothing, Elisha was insistent on doing something for this woman." So, he called her again and said, "About this time next year, you will hold a son in your arms." When you make room, God will make room for all of the things that He desires for you to have.

Focus on **Proverbs 18:16** "A man's gift maketh room for him, and bringeth him before great men."

Exercise: Remove three items out of your physical closet and bless someone else. First, pray over the items, and ask God who you should bless with the special items. Next, remove one thing in your life that is keeping you from opening up to new opportunities.

What items are you removing? Explain the reason why you decided to remove them.

_____

_____

_____

_____

_____

_____

_____

_____

_____

_____

_____

_____

_____

_____

_____

_____

_____

_____

15

A Saved Remnant

Romans 9: 27-28

[27] "Isaiah cries out concerning Israel: "Though the number of the Israelites be like the sand by the sea, only the remnant will be saved.[28] For the Lord will carry out his sentence on earth with speed and finality."

A remnant is a "leftover amount" or "what is left from a large portion of food, materials, groups or people." Some people look at remnants as scraps or things that are worthless, but to God, remnants have value. They are set aside for His holy purpose. For example, God will continue to remove things out of your life. He will reveal what is most important and what is not, but the remnant He has purged, He also gives value. You are the remnant set aside to be used by God for His glory.

The remnant is the minority, and the rest are considered the majority. We must always remember that remnants are small. You are not meant to have everyone around you. It only takes a small group of people to push you into your destiny. When you are set apart, it's not meant for you to include everyone in your personal time with God.

Whatever remains after the battle is what God has ordained for you. We, the body of Christ, are God's remnant of people, saved by grace. You are a remnant. You are unshakable; you are loved and are set apart.

In what ways does the passage below apply to you as a remnant of God?

Matthew 7:13-14 "Enter through the narrow gate. For wide is the gate and broad is the road that leads to destruction, and many enter through it. [14] But small is the gate and narrow the road that leads to life, and only a few find it."

_____

_____

_____

_____

_____

_____

_____

_____

_____

_____

_____

_____

_____

_____

_____

_____

_____

_____

_____

_____

16

Your Act of Courage Will Encourage Someone Else

Exodus 1:17

"The midwives, however, feared God and did not do what the king of Egypt had told them to do; they let the boys live."

The book of Exodus provides several examples of chains of courage. A chain of courage is when one fearless act prompts another person's actions, which can change history. For instance, Shiphrah and Puah, the midwives in Egypt, were commanded by Pharaoh to kill all the male children as soon as they were born. However, the midwives feared God, so they did not do what Pharaoh had commanded them to do. Instead, they let the boys live. After giving birth, Jochebed, the mother of Moses hid him for several months in her home. When she could no longer keep his existence a secret, she put him in a basket and placed the basket in the Nile River. Miriam, Moses' sister stood by and watched the basket float away. Pharaoh's daughter then saw the basket and asked that the basket be brought to her. Miriam stepped up and gave suggestions on how to take care of Moses. Had these events not taken place, the course of history would have changed, but Shiphrah and Puah's courage was displayed when they were willing to obey God rather than man.

As a child of God, you have to come to a realization that what you go through is not only for you but for those who are watching your walk in that situation. God uses your testimony to help deliver others. What if you had given up and lay there and died? History cannot be changed when you give up.

Reflect: Look back at your life and reflect on the things that God has delivered you from. Now use that same information to encourage the next person. God gave you a testimony to help the next person, but you must build up enough courage to release that information. Your courage can help others that are in deep situations.

How have those things or people that were delivered changed your life?

_____

_____

_____

_____

_____

_____

_____

_____

_____

_____

_____

_____

_____

_____

_____

_____

_____

17

Good Morning: Wake Up

Psalm 30:5

"For his anger endureth but a moment; in his favour is life: weeping may endure for a night, but joy cometh in the morning."

The Bible says that weeping may endure for a night, but joy comes in the morning. Have you ever been going through a situation, went to bed and awoke the next morning thinking that everything would be okay, just to find out that nothing had changed. Therefore, you continue day by day and awake morning by morning: worrying, struggling and trying to figure things out. Then you begin to ask God when your "morning" will come. "When will I be relieved of this issue and the hell that I'm in?" God is telling you, "Your morning is right now. Your morning is when you wake up." It has nothing to do with AM or PM. When you give God your family, your bills, all of your worries and you leave it alone. God is telling you, "WAKE UP and GOOD MORNING." Your morning can happen at noon, 5 pm, 8 pm, or 11 pm. It is the moment the light comes on inside your head. Your joy is waiting on you. Let God fight that battle. Once you let it go, you will have your joy. Your joy can begin right now; your morning can begin right now, if you just wake up.

Too many times, we miss our morning because we are too worried. Today, I decree and declare that you will not miss another "morning." For about ten years, I missed my "morning" and my joy because I constantly worried about an issue, but when I finally let it go, BOY did I have joy. Everyone deserves to feel that gracious joy. SO, WAKEUP!

Refection: Is there anything you are holding on to that you have been weeping about? If so, begin to hand it over to God so that you may receive your joy.

What was your wakeup call?

_____

_____

_____

_____

_____

_____

_____

_____

_____

_____

_____

_____

_____

_____

_____

_____

_____

_____

_____

_____

_____

18

Let go of any Battles that are not Yours

Exodus 14:14

"The Lord will fight for you, and you have only to be silent. "

2 Chronicles 20:17

"You will not have to fight this battle. Take up your positions; stand firm and see the deliverance the LORD will give you, Judah and Jerusalem. Do not be afraid; do not be discouraged. Go out to face them tomorrow, and the LORD will be with you. "

There will always be battles we will face in life. They can range from health issues to financial issues. Jesus died on the cross so that we can overcome them all. But not all are meant for us to fight in the flesh. In fact, it is impossible for us to fight a spiritual war in fleshly form. Sometimes, God will fight the battle through you, but there are times God wants to step in and fight the battle for you. All you have to do is position yourself by praying. Then watch God work. There is nothing you will have to worry about because "No weapon that is formed against you shall prosper."

God will remove the attack that is coming against you. This is where God will display His power and ensure that He is in complete control. While God is fighting your battles, utilize the weapons that he has given you, prayer and the Word. So, do not spend time worrying about things that are out of your control. Confuse the enemy by worshipping and praising God in the midst of your battle.

King Jehoshaphat is an excellent example in 2 Chronicles 20. He was going up against several enemies. At first, he was worried, but then he sought God. He sought after God and waited to hear God's plan. God then sent prophets to speak to Jehoshaphat. Verses 17-19 of 2 Chronicles reads, "You will not have to fight this battle. Judah and Jerusalem, take up your positions; stand firm, and you will see the deliverance the LORD will give you. Do not be afraid; do not be discouraged. Go out to face them tomorrow, and the LORD will be with you. Jehoshaphat bowed down with his face to the ground, and all the people of Judah and Jerusalem fell down in worship before the LORD. Then some Levites from the Kohathites and Korahites stood up and praised the LORD, the God of Israel, with a very loud voice. ''

When God says, "I got you" break out in praise for what He is about to do. You have to be preemptive in your praise and worship and not worry about this situation. Although God is fighting your battle, you will still face that issue head-on, but He only asks you to take your position, stand firm, and see your deliverance.

What are your thoughts about how Jehoshaphat reacted when it came to the battle?

_____

_____

_____

_____

_____

_____

_____

_____

_____

How do you react when it comes to challenges?

_____

_____

_____

_____

_____

_____

_____

_____

_____

19

The Process and the Transformation

Romans 12:2

"And do not be conformed to this world, but be transformed by the renewing of your mind, so that you may prove what the will of God is, that which is good and acceptable and perfect."

God wants to get the best oil out of you, so you must go through a process. We all know that olive oil comes from olives that have been crushed under pressure. We also know that the main ingredient in Holy oil is Olive oil. It is very interesting why the olive oil was chosen to be the main ingredient. Could it be because of the process and transformation it had to go through to become oil? The oil is only able to flow when the olive is under pressure. Your true anointing can only flow when God puts pressure on you. God is allowing the pressure to produce the truth inside of you and your transformation. Therefore, applied pressure causes God's anointing to come forth.

There is a process to everything. If you want to get to your destiny or to where God wants you to be, there is no way around the process. It is not easy. God is saying to you today, "When you are being pressed, allow the pressing." Understand that you cannot make it through Gethsemane (In Hebrew, this means an olive press) on your strength alone. So, you must watch and pray with full dependence on God and the Holy Spirit. There is no way to mature in Christ without setbacks nor can you speed up the process. The olive tree that develops deep roots can produce fruit for several centuries, but it may take up to 30 years to mature. Allow God to cultivate you like the olive tree. It will not happen overnight. Many people will not recognize your change in the beginning, but eventually, they will see the change in you.

I remember returning to God. I was on fire and ready to dive in head first, but I didn't realize that change is a process. I was still letting go of somethings in my life. I didn't get there overnight, so you won't change overnight. As eager as I was, I had to be patient and go through the process. Scripture says, "Be ye transformed by the renewing of your mind." We have to first transform our mind to want to change before we can change.

We must go through a metamorphosis. Think of the stage of a caterpillar changing into a butterfly or a tadpole changing into a frog. Each stage is a process of elevation.

We must allow God to wash us through and through during the process. Remember, if you want to be the greatest, you must go through the greatest change with God. Then you will be able to say, "I came, I went, and I conquered."

Using the caterpillar and the tadpole metamorphosis, explain which would suit your change better? Are you a jumper or do you prefer to fly?

_____

_____

_____

_____

_____

_____

_____

_____

_____

_____

_____

_____

_____

_____

_____

_____

_____

_____

_____

_____

20

Saved but not Converted: Submit

Acts 28:27

"For this people's heart have become calloused; they hardly hear with their ears, and they have closed their eyes. Otherwise, they might see with their eyes, hear with their ears, understand with their hearts and turn, and I would heal them."

Submission is the best act of obedience, but so many Christians want salvation without conversion. There are too many believers that are saved but have not submitted their lives to God and the word of God. It takes a lot more than just confessing Jesus as Lord and repenting. The believer must begin to change and conform to the will and Word of God. Submit your body and soul so that God can use you to your fullest potential. God is saying, "Give me you; everything else can wait because I am in control of all things."

Peter started off as an unconverted believer who followed Jesus. It wasn't until Peter saw himself in a different light and was confronted with his own sin and carnal behavior that the conversion began. Peter had not been converted when confronted at the trial of Jesus; he denied he knew the Lord. Peter believed in Jesus and the works that he had done, but that was not enough. Peter eventually became converted and believed in who He was: The Son of God.

No believer can continue living life as normal or lukewarm. You must make a decision; it's either all or nothing. I was driving one day and saw a sign that said "A half of truth is a whole lie." There must be full submission when there is a commitment to God. God did not promise you half of Him. He gives you all of Him. He sent His whole son to die for your sins, so submit and give God all of you. I beseech you to submit today and be led by the Holy Spirit.

There are Christians that have confessed Jesus as Lord and have been saved for years, but most never converted. You are not converted by merely believing in Jesus. In order to become a greater version of you, self-examination is necessary to see if you've truly surrendered your entire life to God. One must be HEARERS and DOERS of God's Word and works.

Examination: Re-examine your life to see if you have completely surrendered every part of it to God. If you find, in your examination, that you have fallen short, begin to repent and ask God how to submit your total being to him?

What areas of your life have you not surrendered?

_____

_____

_____

_____

_____

_____

_____

What will it take for you to surrender? What is hindering your release?

_____

_____

_____

_____

_____

_____

_____

_____

_____

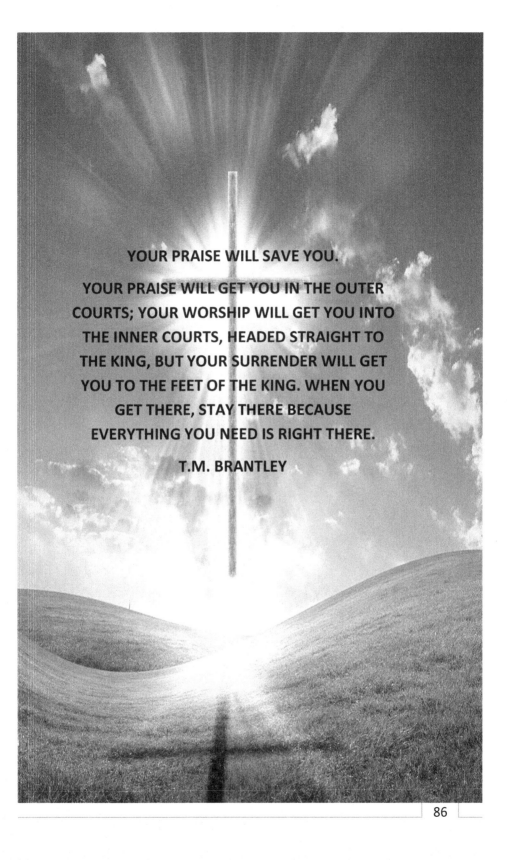

YOUR PRAISE WILL SAVE YOU.

YOUR PRAISE WILL GET YOU IN THE OUTER COURTS; YOUR WORSHIP WILL GET YOU INTO THE INNER COURTS, HEADED STRAIGHT TO THE KING, BUT YOUR SURRENDER WILL GET YOU TO THE FEET OF THE KING. WHEN YOU GET THERE, STAY THERE BECAUSE EVERYTHING YOU NEED IS RIGHT THERE.

T.M. BRANTLEY

21

Your Hurt Makes Me Happy: Circumstances

Isaiah 41:10

"Do not fear, for I am with you; do not be dismayed, for I am your God. I will strengthen you, I will help you, yes, I will uphold you with My righteous right hand."

2 Corinthians 1:3-4

"Blessed be God, the Father of our Lord Jesus Christ, the Father of mercies, and the God of all comfort, who comforts us in all our tribulation, that we may be able to comfort those who are in any trouble by the comfort with which we ourselves are comforted by God."

God must have first place in your heart. The believer's desire must align with God's will and his purpose. God delights in His children and He wants to give you the desires of your heart, but sometimes, before you get to those stages, you have to go through the rough patches in life. These may be from decisions we have made, but it's okay. There is always a process that must happen to transition. For example, you may have been hurt in a relationship or may have been abused. These may be situations that God had warned you about, and you decided to continue. Finally, the situation is over, and you are feeling lonely and depressed, but you know you must go through the pain to get better.

Your hurt makes me happy. I am not happy about what has happened, but I am happy about the hurt that is leading you to your change. I know that through your hurt your purpose will be produced, testimonies are being written, and businesses are being developed. God did not take you through the hurting process for nothing. There is a reason, but it's all about what you decide to do with the new you and the revelation that God has given to you. Because of our sin, Calvary was produced, so imagine what your pain and hurt can produce in you. That is why your hurt makes me happy; you have the power to change your circumstances. If you can't change your circumstances, change your environment and possibly the people around you, but don't forget to allow God to lead you.

Psalms 119:67 "Before I was afflicted, I went astray, but now I have kept thy Word."

In your words, what does **Psalms 119:67** means?

_____

_____

_____

_____

_____

_____

_____

_____

_____

_____

_____

_____

_____

_____

_____

_____

_____

_____

_____

_____

22

Before you want more, don't forget about what you already have

Numbers 11:4-6

[4]"The rabble with them began to crave other food, and again the Israelites started wailing and said, 'If only we had meat to eat! [5]We remember the fish we ate in Egypt at no cost—also the cucumbers, melons, leeks, onions and garlic. [6]But now we have lost our appetite; we never see anything but this manna!'

We can get selfish…very selfish. There are times we get to a point when we are not satisfied with what we already have. God lead the people of Israel out of bondage in Egypt. After all that he had done, all they could do was complain about what they wanted but did not have. The scriptures state that they had food, but they didn't have meat, so they were not satisfied. Sometimes, we have to think back on what God has already given us until we are in a position to receive more. Be thankful for the vegetables and fruit because you are not going hungry.

Be thankful for the apartment until your time has come for you to receive a house. Be thankful for being able to ride the train or bus to work because when you are in the right position, God will bless you with a car. So, before you want more, don't forget about what you already have. You don't want to go and purchase a car in your current situation because your income may not be able to support it. Be grateful and position yourself for the time that God will bless you.

Reflection: Begin to measure your life based on God's standards. Are there things that God has blessed you with, and you have taken them for granted? Are there things that you have, yet you want more? If so, begin to write your vision and get yourself in position to receive what God has for you.

_____

_____

_____

_____

_____

_____

_____

_____

_____

_____

_____

_____

_____

_____

_____

_____

_____

_____

_____

_____

_____

_____

23

Raise your P-Raise

Psalms 149 :1-9

[1]"Praise the LORD. Sing to the LORD a new song, his praise in the assembly of his faithful people. [2]Let Israel rejoice in their Maker; let the people of Zion be glad in their King.[3]Let them praise his name with dancing and make music to him with timbrel and harp. [4]For the LORD takes delight in his people; he crowns the humble with victory.[5]Let his faithful people rejoice in this honor and sing for joy on their beds.[6]May the praise of God be in their mouths and a double-edged sword in their hands,[7]to inflict vengeance on the nations and punishment on the peoples,[8]to bind their kings with fetters, their nobles with shackles of iron [9]to carry out the sentence written against them; this is the glory of all his faithful people. Praise the LORD. "

Psalms 148:1-4

"Praise ye the LORD. Praise ye the LORD from the heavens: praise him in the heights. Praise ye him, all his angels: praise ye him, all his hosts. Praise ye him, sun and moon: praise him, all ye stars of light. Praise him, ye heavens of heavens, and ye waters that be above the heavens."

Hallelujah is the highest praise, but there are levels to your praise. There is a reason why praise has the word raise embedded in it. While praising God, you should ascend through different levels. Each level should be more intense. As you develop your relationship with God, or as you experience different trials, you will need to raise your praise. You must continue to go higher in your praise because God is going to help rip away layers as you exalt His name. Your praise will rip layers off of your past, rip layers from hurt, broken hearts, and sickness.

God wants you to come up higher, but you must stop allowing issues and circumstances to block you from raising your praise. You must face your circumstances head on and praise God in the midst of them. "You are a chosen people, a royal priesthood, a holy nation, a people belonging to God, *that you may declare the praises of Him* who called you out of darkness into his wonderful light," 1 Peter 2:9. You are called and chosen for the purpose of praising and worshipping God. Get in a place where you can see and feel God because it is guaranteed that God will reveal himself to you.

Exercise

During this time begin to block out everything and everyone around you. This is the time for your intense praise. Do not ask God for anything, and do not pray for anyone, just praise Him for who He is in your life. Make sure your praise is so intense that you go to another level in Him. Ask God what you can do for him. Allow God's presence to consume your house by using the greatest weapon of warfare, your praise. **To enter your next level in God, your password is Praise.** Don't forget to journal.

How do you feel after your encounter?

_____

_____

_____

_____

_____

_____

_____

_____

_____

_____

_____

_____

_____

_____

24

You Can't Run from God

❖ . . . . ❖

Jonah 1: 1-3

¹ "The word of the LORD came to Jonah, son of Amittai: ²'Go to the great city of Nineveh and preach against it, because its wickedness has come up before me.' ³But Jonah ran away from the LORD and headed for Tarshish. He went down to Joppa, where he found a ship bound for that port. After paying the fare, he went aboard and sailed for Tarshish to flee from the LORD. "

God has called you to a higher position. You have already been qualified for what He called you to do. Often times we run from our calling and we go in a different direction. When God has His hand on your life, He will not leave you alone. You may find yourself in a place of loneliness or confinement. Sometimes you are directed to go west, and you decide to go east. Understand that you cannot run forever. God will begin to shake some things up in your life. **He will pull you from what you are running to and pull you back to what you are running from.**

Jonah was told to go to Nineveh, but instead he decided to get on a boat for Tarshish. The word says "He was fleeing from the presence of the Lord." God wasn't going to allow him to run forever, so the Lord sent a storm which could have caused the ship to be broken. The crew was afraid and called each man to call on his god for them to reach safety. Jonah confessed to the men that it was probably his fault as to why they were in the dilemma. The crew then tossed him overboard, and he was swallowed by a big fish. God will show you who is around you and how they really feel about you, when they feel they are in jeopardy of dying or losing something. Understand this, your crew, the people you trust, the people that are supposed to have your back, may not hesitate to sacrifice you to save themselves.

God will put you in a position where you will have to seek him. Jonah turned to God and prayed unto Him from the belly of the fish, from the inside of his place of confinement. When you are in your most raw and desperate state, you will stop running and turn back to God. Jonah was in the belly of the fish for three days and three nights before God delivered him. Even though Jonah did not follow God's direction, Jonah's calling and purpose did not change. It was just delayed because of disobedience. When you have a calling on your life, God will not leave you alone, although you may feel alone.

Reflection: For the next three days, if there is anything that you are running from, face it, and stop running. I challenge you to trust God and go in the direction that He tells you to go.

Explain your experience for the next three days.

Day 1

_____

_____

_____

_____

_____

_____

Day 2

_____

_____

_____

_____

_____

_____

Day 3

_____

_____

_____

_____

_____

_____

25

You Were not Designed to Stay Broken

Psalm 51:17

"My sacrifice, O God, is a broken spirit; a broken and contrite heart you, God, will not despise. "

Brokenness is an uncomfortable feeling, and it can take you into a place of darkness. You must learn to allow God to be that light in your dark place. No one is ever exempt from being broken, but you can't make it your home. Rule number one: never stay in your brokenness because of convenience or loyalty. God wants us to be loyal to Him and conform to His will. If it is blocking you from His will, you must seek God for deliverance. Rule number two: if you are broken, don't stay too long. Being broken can cause further issues-- issues such as mistrust or illnesses. Being broken may separate you from God, and may sometimes cause death. You want to go through this with God and allow Him to deliver you. Rule number three: don't try to do it by yourself.

Every so often we try to mend ourselves by playing the doctor. You can't use a bandage or put super glue on it and think everything is okay. Being stressed or having a lot of pressure on you will cause another break. The things mentioned above are not strong enough to mend the type of brokenness you may be experiencing. Seek God and allow Him to mend you. If you allow God to guide you, trust me when I say, there will always be something good to come out of a bad situation. God wants you to be whole, that is why He sent His son to die for your sins. The enemy did not have the power or the authority to break Jesus, so the enemy doesn't have the power nor the authority to break you. You were not designed to be broken. You were not designed to stay broken; you were designed to be whole.

Always remember that you cannot control how people act toward you, but you can control how you react to them. Don't allow anything, anyone or any type of brokenness to come between you and God. Understand that God will not cast you out for being broken, but He doesn't want you to stay there. He wants you whole with nothing missing. Turn your brokenness into something good. Learn the lesson and get out. You can only do this with God. Begin to re-evaluate your life and if there are any broken areas lift your hands to God and say, "I need you."

Reflection: If there are any broken areas in your life or if you know anybody dealing with brokenness, began to call them out. Being broken is not bad but staying will allow you to rot away. The prophecy was fulfilled the day of crucifixion when the guards did not break Jesus' legs. The legs of the sacrificial lamb didn't break. This is proof that brokenness is not permanent.

How are you dealing with brokenness in your life and others' lives?

_____

_____

_____

_____

_____

_____

_____

_____

_____

_____

_____

_____

_____

_____

_____

_____

26

Water to Wine: The Mandate

◈ · · · · · · · · · · · · · · · · · · ◈

John 2:7-9

[7] "Jesus said to the servants, 'Fill the jars with water"; so they filled them to the brim.[8] Then he told them, "Now draw some out and take it to the master of the banquet.' They did so, [9] and the master of the banquet tasted the water that had been turned into wine. He did not realize where it had come from, though the servants who had drawn the water knew. Then he called the bridegroom aside. "

All God is telling you to do is pour the water, and He will make the wine. Take one step, and He will make the next. Be obedient and you won't have to sacrifice anything. When God leads you to do something, DO IT, even if it doesn't seem right or if you don't understand from where the resources will come. Do your part, and He will perform a miracle in your life. Keep standing and know that God will continue to lift you up. God is preparing you to fulfill a mandate, so the process is critical. He has given you the go ahead, but you must do your part and not try to do the miracle.

Moses' mandate was to free the people from Israel. He understood his assignment and was willing to risk his life to complete the mandate. Moses poured his water by following Gods orders and going to Egypt. The mandate was fulfilled by freeing the people of Israel. Understand that you will pour your water several times. In life, you will have to pour out.

Obey God's mandate, continue to pour your water, and in due time, God will turn it into wine. It will be worth the wait, the struggle, the suffering, the pain, and the process.

Is there any area of your life where God is telling you to just pour the water and allow him to make the wine? For example, is there a business, book, or a ministry that He has put in your heart to begin?

_____

_____

_____

_____

_____

_____

_____

_____

_____

_____

_____

_____

_____

_____

_____

_____

_____

_____

_____

_____

27

The Power to Stand

Philippians 4:13

"For I can do everything through Christ, who gives me strength."

Isaiah 41:10

"Don't be afraid, for I am with you. Don't be discouraged, for I am your God. I will strengthen you and help you. I will hold you up with my victorious right hand. "

When you come to a point in your life where all hell is breaking loose, you must call on the name of Jesus and stand. There is so much power running through your veins that will not allow you to fall nor give up. During difficult times, cling to the Lord and His promises. Understand that trials can draw us nearer to God.

We have all dealt with relationship issues, whether family, friends, in marriage or a relationship with a significant other. We can get so involved, and when it begins to unravel and come to an end, we don't know how to let go. We risk our heart, our love, and our time. God is saying, "Trust me and know that in me you can stand through anything."

God has given me the power to stand in the midst of any storm. I don't have to run for cover or shelter because He keeps me, as I keep my eyes on Him. I have been talked about to the point where people tried to assassinate my character. I have been told that my hair wasn't long enough; I wasn't pretty enough; I was too dark, and I wasn't skinny enough. Words do hurt, and they can damage a person to the core. When you have the power of God in your life, you can stand against anyone or anything. I may not be perfect for you, but I am perfectly imperfect for God.

I will stand until it's time for me to bow. Regardless of my circumstances and my situations I will trust God to help me stand. I am not powerless I am powerful.

Do not walk around with your tools and not activate the power. As long as you have Jesus on your side, he is the only tool you need.

God has given you the power to stand against all things. What is keeping you from activating that power?

_____

_____

_____

_____

_____

_____

_____

_____

_____

_____

_____

_____

_____

_____

_____

_____

_____

_____

_____

28

Grace Rewrote my Life Story

Genesis 6:3-8.

[5] "The LORD saw how great the wickedness of the human race had become on the earth, and that every inclination of the thoughts of the human heart was only evil all the time. [6] The LORD regretted that he had made human beings on the earth, and his heart was deeply troubled. [7] So the LORD said, "I will wipe from the face of the earth the human race I have created—and with them the animals, the birds and the creatures that move along the ground— for I regret that I have made them." [8] But Noah found favor in the eyes of the LORD."

2 Corinthians 12:9

"But he said to me, "My grace is sufficient for you, for my power is made perfect in weakness." Therefore, I will boast all the more gladly about my weaknesses, so that Christ's power may rest on me."

Oh Lord, where would we be if it were not for your grace? Grace can redeem your life when you think it is over. God, our father, has given us grace and mercy.

The word grace in Hebrew means kindness and favor, and in the Greek, it means mercy and favor. The first sign of grace was when Noah found grace in the sight of the Lord. This took place in Genesis 6:8 when the Lord saw how great the wickedness had become on the earth. The Lord was disappointed that He had made man, and He was grieved in His heart. God had made the decision to destroy all men and beast from the earth, but He saw Noah and Noah found grace in His eyes. Noah was a great and just man that walked with God. At that moment, grace re-wrote his destiny because he was now on assignment for the Lord.

Not everyone has a story like Noah, but we all have a story on how God has shown grace toward us, and we did not deserve it. God has given us a divine pardon and has canceled out all judgment that could have come against us.

Your life was spared because of God's grace. You have no excuse to not be the greatest you. Grace is the unmerited favor of God, and his grace is sufficient.

Focus: Think back on how "grace" rewrote your life and how blessed you have been. When God could have given up on you, he didn't. God's grace is nothing you deserve, nothing you earn, but you would be lost without it.

What is your story of "grace?"

_____

_____

_____

_____

_____

_____

_____

_____

_____

_____

_____

_____

_____

_____

_____

_____

_____

_____

_____

_____

29

Anointed to Finish

John 17:18

"As you sent me into the world, I have sent them into the world."

Ecclesiastes 9:11

"I have seen something else under the sun: The race is not to the swift or the battle to the strong, nor does food come to the wise or wealth to the brilliant or favor to the learned; but time and chance happen to them all."

When God has anointed, appointed, qualified, and called you, there is no person, no devil, nor any issue that can stop God's plan for your life. God has anointed you for a reason and for His purpose. That purpose has an assignment that needs to be accomplished. Your assignment comes directly from God. God sent His only begotten son on a mission, and He continued until it was completed on the cross. We, as the Kingdom of God, have our own assignment

God gave Abram an assignment to leave his homeland and become the father of many nations. God gave Moses an assignment to lead the people to the Promised Land. Jesus was on assignment to die for our sins. What if they did not complete their assignment? I'm sure it wasn't easy, and they may have questioned why, but God will make sure that you are anointed for that task so that you can complete your assignment.

Too many times, we became distracted from completing an assignment that God appointed us to do. Those things could have been self-issues such as identity. I used to be guilty of quitting because I always worried about who would not receive me or what they would say about me. I now remind myself that Jesus was not exempt from being talked about, so I must continue on with my assigned purpose.

If you are having issues, ask God to reveal your purposed assignment. Ask God what you need to do? If you know your assignment and you are struggling to complete it, find out what is keeping from your purpose.

If it's people, you may have to release them or separate yourself. Do not allow anything to block you from fulfilling your purpose, which will soon produce your blessings.

Someone is waiting on you. In addition, you may be waiting for your deliverance that is being hindered by not completing the assignment. The greatest part of you is on the other side of your completed assignment, so go and get what God has for you.

What is your purposed assignment, and do you feel like you are anointed to finish? Why?

_____

_____

_____

_____

_____

_____

_____

_____

_____

_____

_____

_____

_____

_____

_____

_____

_____

_____

_____

_____

_____

_____

_____

30

Wait and Stop Trying to Understand

Psalms 27:14

"Wait on the LORD: be of good courage, and he shall strengthen thine heart: wait, I say, on the LORD."

John 13:7

"Jesus replied 'You do not realize now what I am doing, but later you will understand.'"

Have you ever rushed into a relationship or job because you got tired of waiting on God? Then you found yourself in a bad position because of your decisions. Aren't you tired of making your own plans in your own timing? Aren't you tired of failing? Isn't it time to wait on the Lord? No one likes to wait. Yes, I know it may be one of your most difficult tasks, but waiting will remind you that you are not in charge; God is in control. We may not see God working in our lives, but in such times, we must understand that He is always working.

The rewards that God can bestow upon your life are far greater than what you can do out of your own flesh. Never be anxious for anything. Continue to allow God to bring the things He desires for your life. God is the only one that knows your true, divine calling. You do not have to understand God's plan for your life at this moment, but you will soon. God wants you to live a life that will be recorded in heaven, not on earth. As you wait on God to bring that job, husband, wife, house or anything you desire, trust Him and have faith that He will do it. He will do it in His timing. Patiently wait and remember Apostle Peter's words, "That with the Lord one day is like a thousand years." After all that has occurred in your life, wait. Wait on the Lord for He knows the plans He has for your life much better than you. Know that unanswered questions are a big part of trusting God.

Reflection: Ask yourself, do you want to work on your timing to receive small rewards that will perish the moment you are deceased? Or would you rather allow God to do things in his timing so that He can apply His perfect will for you to receive the full reward, which will last forever?

_____

_____

_____

_____

_____

_____

_____

_____

_____

_____

_____

_____

_____

_____

_____

_____

_____

_____

_____

_____

_____

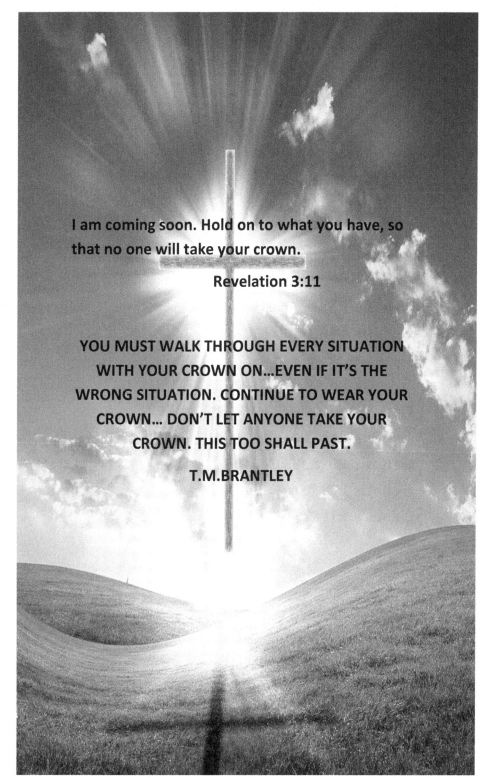

I am coming soon. Hold on to what you have, so that no one will take your crown.

Revelation 3:11

YOU MUST WALK THROUGH EVERY SITUATION WITH YOUR CROWN ON...EVEN IF IT'S THE WRONG SITUATION. CONTINUE TO WEAR YOUR CROWN... DON'T LET ANYONE TAKE YOUR CROWN. THIS TOO SHALL PAST.

T.M.BRANTLEY

31

Sometimes you have to go back to the Beginning: God doesn't need your help

Genesis 1:1 "In the beginning, God created the heavens and the earth…"
Genesis 1:3 "And God said…"
Genesis 1:4 "God Saw…"
Genesis 1: 5 "God called…"
Genesis 1:6 "And God said…"
Genesis 1:7 "So God made…"
Genesis 1:8 "God called…"
Genesis 1:9 "And God said…"
Genesis 1:10 "God called…"
Genesis 1:11 "Then God said…And so on."

John 1:1-5

[1] "In the beginning was the Word, and the Word was with God, and the Word was God. [2] He was with God in the beginning. [3] Through him all things were made; without him nothing was made that has been made. [4] In him was life, and that life was the light of all mankind. [5] The light shines in the darkness, and the darkness has not overcome it."

Sometimes you have to stop looking for resources and look at the source. It is okay to go back to Genesis and start over. The first thing you have to understand is that Genesis states, "In the beginning, God created," not you and God created. That means that He never needed your help. When you are done failing by following your own plan, go back to the beginning and allow God to create the path and steps in your life. As humans, we want to be involved in things that are concerning us, but we don't realize we don't have the skills to negotiate on our behalf. So, when we get involved, we mess it all up. Everything you start should begin and end with God, not with you or any other person. God is God all by himself. He created the earth and everything that dwells in it. God made you and me, so why do you feel He needs help solving your problems. Stop getting involved with God's business and allow him in your business.

When you feel exhausted and there is nowhere for you to go, you may feel that you are in between a rock and a hard place. You may have been running into brick walls. Just return to the beginning and consult with the creator. Nothing will be lost by starting over. This is one thing I love about God. He gives us the opportunity to make our own decisions and gives us the grace to start over. He is a God of a second, third and fourth chance. I pray that these last few days were the start of your new beginning. I pray that they added balance to your life. I pray that God will reveal everything that He wants you to know and that you will obedient to God's demands.

How many times did you have to return to the beginning?

_____

_____

_____

_____

_____

Did you feel like it was a waste of time following your own plan?

_____

_____

_____

_____

_____

What did you learn during this time?

_____

_____

_____

_____

_____

Remember that God is the negotiator. What are you trying to negotiate with God?

_____

_____

_____

_____

_____

32

Beauty is Only Skin Deep

Proverbs 31:30

Favour is deceitful, and beauty is vain: but a woman that feareth the LORD, she shall be praised."

We were always taught that beauty was external, but true beauty is internal. Have you ever seen a person who was absolutely gorgeous on the outside? They may have a great body, pretty hair, and can get any man or woman they want, but they have issues. They may have arrogant and cocky ways. It doesn't matter how pretty or handsome you are on the outside. If your inside is rotten, then you, as a whole, are rotten.

There are people who may be insecure or have low self-esteem. This is because the world defines beauty, and if they don't fit in a certain category, that causes people to want to change how they look. The world defines beauty by body type, hair, lips, legs and butt. However, God looks at your heart, which determines your character.

God says, "You are more than enough because I am more than enough." It doesn't matter what society say about who or what you are supposed to be. You are enough. Your heart is more than enough. Your love is more than enough, your personality is more than enough. God made you in his image, so it doesn't matter what you can produce or how much money you have. It has nothing to do with looks, but you alone are ENOUGH. Who are you going to believe--God or Man (Society)? Continue to work on this. God is not concerned about your physical looks, he is concerned about how your heart looks.

Pretty is not enough…our hearts must be in the right posture.

Remember, we serve a more than enough God.

Have you ever felt as if you were not good enough? If so, what were your feelings?

_____

_____

_____

_____

_____

_____

_____

Did you overcome that feeling?

Yes   No

☐   ☐

Explain how you overcame? Or explain why and how you did not overcome?

_____

_____

_____

_____

_____

_____

Write yourself a positive note for the future. If I ever experience that again, I..

_____

_____

_____

_____

_____

_____

33

Testimony: Your Pain, Their Deliverance

Revelation 12:11

"And they overcame him by the blood of the Lamb, and by the word of their testimony; and they loved not their lives unto the death."

The Bible says that we are overcome by our testimony. Many do not understand that their testimony is a gateway to deliverance, not only for you, but for others who have been through or are going through similar situations. There are so many people who are searching for silent help, people who are going through in secret. Their family and friends may not know what they are enduring, but if they can hear your testimony that may be enough for them to get the deliverance they are seeking. We do not go through only for our lessons and growth but to help others on their journey.

For several years, I would not tell my testimony. I was embarrassed but most of all I did not want the sympathy. I didn't want people to look at me as if I was worthless or weak. When I finally listened to God and talked about my experience with cancer, I met a lot of people who went through or was going through their own sickness, and they had never discussed it. My testimony brought comfort to them, and it truly revealed that God was still working miracles. I was healed and made whole. Although my story was unique, it brought life to those who felt as if it was a death sentence for them.

God uses us on this earth to be his walking evidence. Therefore, we have to tell our testimonies when God instructs us because someone is depending on us to get them to the next step in their journey. Do not hold on to the things of God. Your life is not your own; you are his miracle and proof that he is alive and working.

Your testimony will also help you release things you are holding on to. Your testimony can hinder you, or it can help you, the longer you hold on to it. Share your testimony. It will prove that you trust God because you are revealing vital, intimate pieces of your life. There may be people who will take the information and use it against you, but there are people that will thank you because you have helped lift them over a hurdle.

God is pleased when you tell your testimony. You are giving him the glory! It gives reverence to who he truly is, and it proves the doubter wrong. You are overcome by your testimony. Others are also overcome by your testimony. God does not take us through situations to keep us silent. He may have used it to get your attention, to show you and others that he is still on the throne, and that we may use our testimony to save others. I personally understand the pain a person goes through during their test, but it is all for a reason. The struggle will be null and void if you keep it to yourself. God wants you to share it so that others may hear of his works.

Have you ever been scared or reluctant to tell your testimony?

Yes

☐

No

☐

Tell your testimony

_____

_____

_____

_____

_____

_____

_____

_____

_____

_____

_____

_____

_____

_____

_____

_____

_____

_____

_____

_____

_____

_____

34

All or Nothing

◈ · ◈

Matthew 16: 24-25

24 "Then said Jesus unto his disciples, 'If any man will come after me, let him deny himself, and take up his cross, and follow me. 25 For whosoever will save his life shall lose it: and whosoever will lose his life for my sake shall find it."

Do you really give God your all? Hmmm, now that is truly something to ponder. When we are in a relationship, we give it our all. From the beginning, we may say, "Give me all or nothing." No one wants to waste their time on something that is not worth it or build a life on false hopes or lies. Every day we sing songs that minister to us. They are a representation of how we feel about God and the things he is doing in our lives. We may sing, "God I surrender all, I give myself away, withholding nothing," or we may say, "I am your servant, I die daily, use me as you will, I am your willing vessel, I will not speak anything that is not from you."

As you make those kinds statements, how serious are you? Or is it just a nice tune, melody or a cliché. The songs and statements sound good, but do you truly understand what you are asking God to do?

We usually find out when we are challenged, but once we make that declaration unto God, he will use us as he desires. Giving God all simply means to decrease so that he is increased in our lives.

1. Deny: 'No' to self ; 'Yes' to God

Denying self requires giving up anything that would hinder you from doing the will of God. Take your wants and desires down from the throne and place Jesus and his will as the governing power in your life.

2. Take up your cross daily

You have to go through crucifying experiences. Somethings can only be handled by dying. Somethings must die in your life so that new things can grow.

3. Follow me: Your place of discipleship

Don't deceive yourself into thinking you can follow Jesus without first denying yourself and carrying your cross daily.

John 8:12, "Jesus said to the people, 'I am the light of the world. If you follow me, you won't be stumbling through the darkness, because you will have the light that leads to life.'"

When you choose to follow God, you will begin to see light in darkness and things and people that are not of God will fall off, break away, or loose themselves from you. They will shed like old skin.

Understand that everyone cannot handle the trip that God is about to send you on. They are not equipped to go on the assignment that is prepared for your season. But you must make the decision on which side you are on. You may have asked yourselves at some point, "Do I really need to give everything to God?" If you go to Revelation 3:16, it states, "Because you are lukewarm neither hot nor cold I am about to spit you out my mouth...I wish you were either one or the other. You can't serve two masters." God would rather you be against him than halfheartedly for him. So, either you are in or out, hot or cold; there is no middle ground. Or like my daddy always said, "Go big or go home." If you are not going to do it big, then don't do it at all.

Have you given up total control to God to govern your life?

_____
_____
_____
_____
_____

What is something in your life that needs to die?

_____
_____
_____
_____

What do you need to deny?

_____
_____
_____
_____
_____
_____

What cross do you need to take up daily?

_____
_____
_____
_____
_____
_____
_____
_____
_____

35

What's Inside of your Alabaster?

◈ · ◈

Luke 7:36-38

"And one of the Pharisees desired him that he would eat with him. And he went into the Pharisee's house, and sat down to meat. 37 And, behold, a woman in the city, which was a sinner, when she knew that Jesus sat at meat in the Pharisee's house, brought an alabaster box of ointment, 38 And stood at his feet behind him weeping, and began to wash his feet with tears, and did wipe them with the hairs of her head, and kissed his feet, and anointed them with the ointment."

The alabaster in today's time symbolizes our outer man. Our body is built with a carnal nature; we were born into sin. Once we begin to sit at the feet of Jesus and be transparent, our sins can be forgiven, and they are washed away. During the breaking process is where we become humble and worship the Lord. You are the alabaster, and you are carrying something precious regardless of your sin, but something must happen for the oil to be released.

Something had to happen to the woman, in the scripture, for her to break and pour on to Jesus feet. It very well could have been her sins weighing her down or simple the pressure of life because she was considered a reject, an outcast, sinner, and prostitute. She knew that she needed to break and pour herself out unto Jesus.

You are carrying your alabaster every day. Your body is your temple which is precious. You are sealed with the blood of the lamb, and it is there to prevent us from going crazy or keeps you from being tainted. But when God breaks the alabaster, the house will be filled with your gift and talents. You are releasing things into the atmosphere. Sometimes God keeps you contained until he is ready to use you at the time of your breaking and pouring out. There is no spoilage and no waste when God is using you. But allow him to break you, not your issues. Remember that everything about the alabaster is precious from the body of the container to the oil it holds. You are Precious.

What is contained in your alabaster box?

_____
_____
_____
_____
_____

Are you ready to release what you are carrying around?

_____
_____
_____
_____
_____

How does the story of the woman with the alabaster box compare to your life?

_____
_____
_____
_____
_____
_____
_____
_____
_____

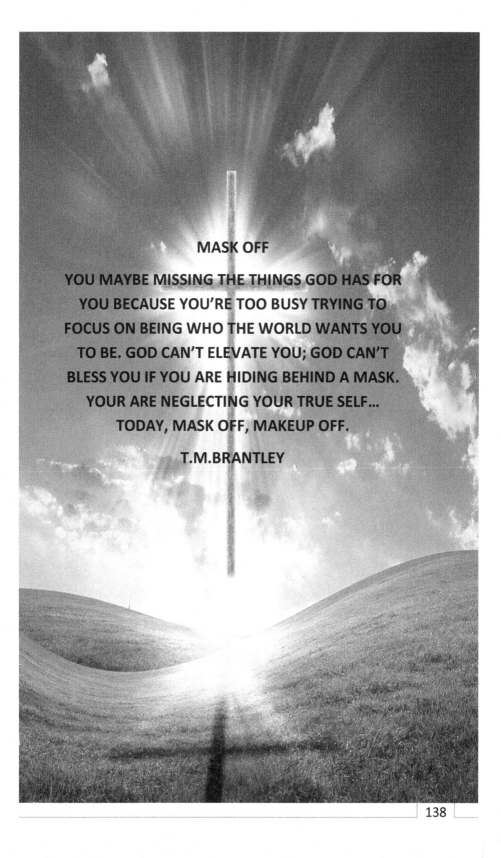

MASK OFF

YOU MAYBE MISSING THE THINGS GOD HAS FOR
YOU BECAUSE YOU'RE TOO BUSY TRYING TO
FOCUS ON BEING WHO THE WORLD WANTS YOU
TO BE. GOD CAN'T ELEVATE YOU; GOD CAN'T
BLESS YOU IF YOU ARE HIDING BEHIND A MASK.
YOUR ARE NEGLECTING YOUR TRUE SELF...
TODAY, MASK OFF, MAKEUP OFF.

T.M.BRANTLEY

36

Chosen for This (He chose you long ago)

John 15:16

"Ye have not chosen me, but I have chosen you, and ordained you, that ye should go and bring forth fruit, and that your fruit should remain: that whatsoever ye shall ask of the Father in My name, He may give it to you."

Matthew 22:14

"For many are called, but few are chosen."

Before your parents knew you, God had already ordained you and created your purpose. He chose you to withstand several difficulties. Please understand, there is a huge difference from being chosen by your family or friends and being chosen by God. When God has put his official stamp of approval on you, it becomes challenging. You now have a target on your back. It seems as if it's you against the world. The devil will pull out all of his tricks. He will use your church. He will use your family; he will use anyone who is close to you. He will try to confuse you about the calling on your life. At that moment, you will know that you have been chosen.

God has chosen and ordained you, but have you accepted the call? Those whom God calls, He justifies. Unless we are justified in the sight of God, we cannot be chosen. Remember, David didn't appear to be qualified. He was cleaning and working with the sheep in the field, and Jessie never considered David. He brought all of his other sons before Samuel. In Jessie's mind, they were more qualified because of what they knew or how they looked, but God chose David and God has chosen you. Many are called, but few are chosen. When Samuel saw David, He said, "He is the one." There are times in your life when people don't want to see you succeed, but the more they don't want you there, guess what, God will send you because He has equipped and ordained you to do the work. You are chosen, but can God depend on you to do the job?

Do you know that you are called?

_____

_____

_____

_____

_____

If so, have you accepted the call?

_____

_____

_____

_____

_____

Is there anything that is hindering you from accepting or walking in your calling?

_____

_____

_____

_____

How does David's story compare to your story?

_____

_____

_____

_____

_____

_____

_____

_____

37

Only God's Opinion Matters

Galatians 1:10

"Am I now trying to win the approval of human beings, or
of God? Or am I trying to please people? If I were still
trying to please people, I would not be a servant of
Christ."

I have always heard the saying "whose report will you believe." It is clear that everyone in your life will have an opinion on how or what you should do about your life and the decisions you have to make. We have to be very careful who we listen to when making these decisions. The world even has their opinion about what is right and what is wrong or how people should act, but if God gave you a clear directive, whose opinion matters?

We search for love in all the wrong places. Then we begin to believe that the world's love is what matters and not God's love. Some of us may be looking for approval, doing things so that people will like us. I once heard a psychologist say, "You need to understand the 20/60/20 rule of people pleasing." He stated that 20 percent of the people you meet immediately like you, 60 percent will straddle the fence, which could be positive or negative, and the other 20 percent will not like you at all.

So, if this is true, why do we spend so much time worrying about others' opinions. God's opinion only matters in your life. Do not put any more energy into what people are saying when God has already given you the blueprint. As you go through life, you will come to realize that everyone will not agree with everything you do. There are people that will pray for your downfall versus praying for you to succeed and make accomplishments. Once again, what God says matters. Get it in your soul so when you stand against your enemy, you will be able to say with power, "Only God's word for my life matters." The Bible is the blueprint for the people who have been told they shouldn't do certain things. If they would have listened to the message in scripture, their outcome would have been different.

Does others' opinions matter to you? How does it make you feel when someone makes a negative comment about you?

_____

_____

_____

_____

_____

_____

_____

_____

Do you allow the opinions formed by others to hinder your day?

_____

_____

_____

_____

_____

_____

Examine your opinions about yourself. Do they block you from your purpose?

_____

_____

_____

_____

_____

_____

38

Get Out of the Way

Isaiah 55:8-9

[8] "For my thoughts are not your thoughts, neither are your ways my ways," declares the LORD. [9]"As the heavens are higher than the earth, so are my ways higher than your ways and my thoughts than your thoughts."

I can remember when I left church due to church hurt. I was at the point where I was tired. I was tired of those who proclaim the name of Jesus but didn't live by the name of Jesus. Everything was glitter and diamonds on the outside, but they were completely different people in their personal lives. The balance of God and living holy lives weren't there. When you are a young adult seeking more of God, and the Christian folks begin to hurt you more than the people in the world, you get stuck. I didn't know enough to continue to push forward. All I knew was that they were not who they proclaimed to be, so I ran. I still had God in my heart, but I didn't want to deal with the church.

> Get out the way of what God is trying to do and show you. At the same time, SHUT UP so you can hear what he is trying to say. Too many times we miss what God is doing and saying because we are our own distraction.

I finally realized that it was not about me, and God had been trying to direct me to the right path for so long, but I kept getting in my own way. God began to bring people in my life that were on fire for him, but I wouldn't accept them because of my past hurt. I couldn't hear what God was telling me because I kept telling myself, "Remember what those Christian people did to you." So, I kept my distance between them and me. I could not move pass the hurt because I kept getting in my own way. I finally surrendered because I was tired of doing it alone. I was able to hear God more clearly. Then I was able to see who he was presenting to me for that season of rebuilding.

I said all of that to say, when you find yourself in a situation with what people have done to you, trust God anyway. The adversary will send anything and anybody as a distraction to get you to turn away from God, but the biggest distraction he uses is your mind. If the enemy can change the way you think, he will control the way you act toward certain situations and people. You will allow they adversary to control if you get in the way of what God is saying to you. GET OUT THE WAY of your deliverance and your freedom. Stop getting distracted by people who were born into sin just as you were. We will all fall short of the glory, but make sure you use discernment. Anytime you find yourself speaking or doing something different from what God declared just say, "Get out of the way, self."

Begin your self-examination. What are you getting in the way of in your life? Are there things you want to do, but you convince yourself not to do them? Put these things in the atmosphere and declare to never get in your own way again.

_____

_____

_____

_____

_____

_____

_____

_____

_____

_____

_____

_____

_____

_____

_____

_____

_____

_____

_____

_____

_____

_____

_____

_____

39

The Doors of the Faithful

Revelation 3:7-13
To the Church in Philadelphia

[7] "To the angel of the church in Philadelphia write:

These are the words of him who is holy and true, who holds the key of David. What he opens no one can shut, and what he shuts no one can open. [8] I know your deeds. See, I have placed before you an open door that no one can shut. I know that you have little strength, yet you have kept my word and have not denied my name. [9] I will make those who are of the synagogue of Satan, who claim to be Jews though they are not, but are liars—I will make them come and fall down at your feet and acknowledge that I have loved you. [10] Since you have kept my command to endure patiently, I will also keep you from the hour of trial that is going to come on the whole world to test the inhabitants of the earth. [11] I am coming soon. Hold on to what you have, so that no one will take your crown. [12] The one who is victorious I will make a pillar in the temple of my God. Never again will they leave it. I will write on them the name of my God and the name of the city of my God, the new Jerusalem, which is coming down out of heaven from my God; and I will also write on them my new name. [13] Whoever has ears, let them hear what the Spirit says to the churches."

The church of Philadelphia was called the faithful church. I wonder how it would feel to be considered faithful by our God. We have to look well into the matter and ask some questions. How were they able to be called faithful as a church? When you are dealing with a church, you are dealing with different personalities, different levels of faith, difference in learning and difference in the way they lived. Jesus wrote letters to the seven churches in revelation and only two churches were considered faithful; this lead me to understand that a faithful church has faithful people. The people of the church of Philadelphia must have had an amazing prayer life and a strong relationship with God to have undeniable faith. In order to have a faithful church, the people have to be faithful in their personal relationship with God, and when they come together corporately, they have faith as a whole. It's all about working together in the kingdom. When we understand that it's not about us individually, then we make things happen.

Due to their faith, they opened doors no man could shut. I don't care how hard people try; they do not have the power nor the authority to close doors that God has opened. No enemy or devil should be able to talk you out of walking away from your God-given door.

God open doors that are everlasting and fulfilling. People and the devil only open temporary doors. Because of your faith, God will open doors for you. Not all doors are meant for you to walk through. Be sure to recognize the door of the Lord because the devil knows what you need as a well, and he doesn't care who he uses to stop or hinder you from reaching your destination.

Have there been any doors you did not walk through because of fear?

_____
_____
_____
_____
_____
_____
_____
_____

Ways to know that your open door is from God:

- God's doors will not come with confusion.
- It will always come with confirmation.
- It will require you to trust him.

Closed doors will sometimes take as much strength and faith as walking through open doors.

How did you handle the closed doors?

_____
_____
_____
_____
_____
_____
_____
_____
_____

40

Declaration of Faith: The Faithful Church

Revelation 3:7
To the Church in Philadelphia

[7] "To the angel of the church in Philadelphia write:

Often time I wonder what if the holy one wrote me a letter. What it would say if he wrote it based on how I live my life today. We all want a Philadelphia letter. I want God to brag and boast on me. I know that I am not perfect, and I definitely fall short of the glory. There are times I may go astray, but I still want my god to be proud of what I am doing in the kingdom and for the kingdom."

Letter to Tina

Well done my child! You have been a good and faithful servant, and because of your faithfulness, I will open doors no man can shut. There will be doors that only you can open…you killed your flesh daily and allowed me to have control. You were persecuted, but I will allow your enemies to bow at your feet (those who claim to be your friends, have lied on you, talked about you, turned their backs on you). They will have no choice but to acknowledge the love I have for you…stay faithful because I will keep you from the hour of trial. Just know I'm coming soon.

- "I know your works" (3:8). You have proven that I can trust you.
- When you didn't know where your healing or strength was coming from, "You have kept My Word and have not denied My name" (3:8).
- I didn't move when you wanted me to, but you endured patiently" (3:10).

So once again hold on and don't let them get the joy of stealing your crown… Well done my Good and faithful servant. You came, you went, and you conquered.

Write a letter based on how you are living your life at this moment. What would God say to you? (be honest with yourself)

Your first letter may not have been the letter you wanted to hear. Write a second letter regarding what you want God to say. This will be something you will strive to do every day of your life.

_____

_____

_____

_____

_____

_____

_____

_____

_____

_____

_____

_____

_____

_____

_____

_____

_____

_____

_____

_____

_____

_____

_____

_____

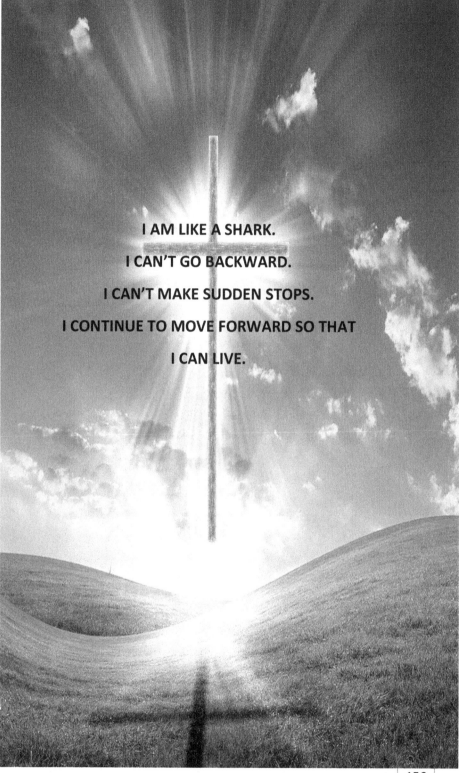

I AM LIKE A SHARK.

I CAN'T GO BACKWARD.

I CAN'T MAKE SUDDEN STOPS.

I CONTINUE TO MOVE FORWARD SO THAT

I CAN LIVE.

I pray that you had a personal encounter with God. I pray that the worrying, the doubt and the pain has ceased. I pray that you have gained confidence, faith and trust, and most importantly, a better relationship with God. Your life should not be the same as it was when you started this consecration. I commend you and pray that your life will forever be changed. Remember that Kingdom life is a blessed life. It gets hard, but thank God that your decisions weren't meant to be final.

2 Chronicles 7: 14

"If my people, which are called by my name, shall humble themselves, and pray, and seek my face, and turn from their wicked ways; then will I hear from heaven, and will forgive their sin, and will heal their land."

NOW YOUR LIFE BEGINS...

Thanks,

I would love to hear about your experience

If you would like to share a written testimony or video recorded testimony, please submit information to ispeakpurpose@gmail.com. Your testimony will bless others.

I AM Greater

I Speak Greatness

I Speak Purpose

You came, You Went, You Conquered

Thank You in Advance

Also visit: http://tmariebrantley.wix.com/tinambrantley

For prayer requests, questions or one-on-one prayer and guidance, please send an email to ispeakpurpose@gmail.com

Made in the USA
Columbia, SC
08 April 2018